· The Naughty and Nice ·
Christmas
Kama Sutra

More than 50 Ways to Have a Merry XXX-Mas

Devorah Lev-Tov
Lindsay Herman

CIDER MILL
PRESS

BOOK
PUBLISHERS

Kennebunkport, Maine

13-Digit ISBN: 978-1604332407
10-Digit ISBN: 1604332409

This book may be ordered by mail from the publisher.
Please include $2.99 for postage and handling.
Please support your local bookseller first!

Books published by Cider Mill Press Book Publishers are available at special discounts for bulk purchases in the United States by corporations, institutions, and other organizations. For more information, please contact the publisher.

Cider Mill Press Book Publishers
"Where good books are ready for press"
12 Port Farm Road
Kennebunkport, Maine 04046

Visit us on the Web!
www.cidermillpress.com

Front cover design by Melissa Gerber
Interior design by Alicia Freile, Tango Media Pty Ltd
Typography: Aphrodite, Archer, Dalliance, and TodaysSB
All illustrations courtesy of Christina Hess
Printed in China

1 2 3 4 5 6 7 8 9 0
First Edition

Contents

Introduction
4

Chapter 1
Antler-to-Antler
8

Chapter 2
Reindeer Style
36

Chapter 3
Open Sleigh
60

Chapter 4
Reindeer Riding
86

Chapter 5
Reckless XXX-Mas
108

Introduction

*A*re you ready to put the XXX back in X-Mas? The Naughty and Nice Christmas Kama Sutra is here for all your holiday-season sexytime needs. While Christmas traditionally emphasizes family time, it's also important to make time to bond with your significant other and celebrate in an intimate and special way. And we're here to help you do just that, one erotic position at a time.

This book is heaving with moves that will really put you in the X-Mas spirit. There are five chapters, each one focusing on a specific style: There's Antler-to-Antler for when you want to be up close and personal. Reindeer-Style is full of sexy rear-entry positions. Open Sleigh features poses with the lady's legs up and spread open. Reindeer Riding puts the woman on top. And Reckless XXX-Mas leans toward the exotic and adventurous, with positions that will have you two experimenting and enjoying yourselves with abandon.

Since some positions are easier to get into than others, we've rated each pose on a difficulty scale of 1 to 5, 1 being easy and 5 being kind of tricky. While 5-rated poses often require some flexibility, they are super fun and a great goal to work up to if you can't quite do them yet. Remember: In the bedroom, practice makes perfect (and it's awfully fun, too!).

We've also offered some helpful variations on each position, labeled as either The Nice Way or The Naughty Way. The Nice Way generally gives a slightly easier or more romantic variation, while The Naughty Way recommends a somewhat more difficult twist on the original pose—or sometimes it's just a little more perverse, for the kinksters! There are also tips for getting into the positions, transitioning into new ones while you're already in the act, and accessorizing for your whoopie sessions.

In addition to the 50-plus positions and variations, we've included creative ideas for spicing up your holiday sex life, whether it's with a Christmas striptease or a naughty little song.

We hope we can help make your holidays a little sexier this year as you treat your partner to an unforgettable Christmas present!

SNOW ANGELS

This move is for the truly wild at heart, and those who can handle the cold. When there's snow on the ground, take your pounding party outside and get into missionary position. As you go at it, swing your arms and legs in and out, creating a sexy snow angel as a testament to your passion.

CHAPTER 1

Antler-
to-Antler

Intense face-to-face action that allows for lots of kissing and eye contact is often what many couples need to experience true intimacy. After all, what time is better than the holiday season to be close to one another? This Christmas you can say goodbye to boring old missionary and hello to merry positions like The Candy Cane, which has the two of you going at it against a wall, and Geese A-Goosing, which puts you in a sideways erotic entanglement. For the more adventurous, find Presents Under the Tree, the Polar Express, and the Bouncing Elf, which will have you in playful postures you'd never thought possible while still facing each other—and you'll be amazed at how much they put you in the holiday spirit!

Mistletoe Mambo

If you're looking to do more than just kiss under the mistletoe this year, grab your partner and seduce him or her into the bedroom where you can have some alone time. This position is a classic for a reason, just be sure to have some mistletoe hanging over the bed!

Get into Position:
The woman lies on her back with her legs spread open. The man lies facedown on top of her and starts the merry motions that will rock her world.

Why It Works:
This quintessential method is easy, direct, and romantic due to the face-to-face potency and closeness of your bodies. It's great for the first time or anytime—especially under some mistletoe.

Difficulty: 1

The Naughty Way: The lady can close her legs and the guy can straddle her, in a kind of inverted (meaning man on top instead of woman on top) version of Rudolph's Ride (page 89).

Accessories: Mistletoe

Silent Night

This position is perfect for when you're home for the holidays—but it's not your home. After all, you don't want to wake Mom and Dad while you're doing the nasty.

Get into Position:
The man lies on his back with his legs slightly open and the woman climbs on top, keeping her legs straight and together. Now just try and keep quiet as the two of you make small but intense movements.

Why It Works:
Trying to keep quiet is always a turn-on; just knowing that you could get "in trouble" is exciting in itself. Couple that with the powerful intimacy of being so close together, and the gentle, slow friction is all you'll need to get to pleasurable heights.

Difficulty: 2

The Naughty Way: To make it even more intoxicating, try tying a scarf over one or both your mouths.

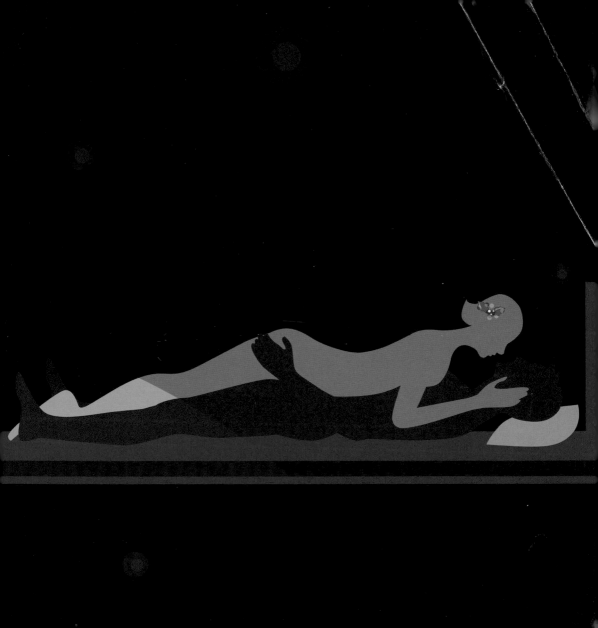

Dashing Through the Snow

Santa's not the only one who can go for a ride on Christmas Eve. In this position the woman can ride her reindeer with wild abandon as he rests comfortably on a bed or chair.

Get into Position:
The man sits on the edge of a bed or chair and the woman sits on his lap facing him, with her legs straddling his waist and her arms on his shoulders.

Why It Works:
This position is great for lots of lip locking, as your faces will be nose to nose. It's super intimate and comfortable for both partners, while still allowing for some prime pumping action.

Difficulty: 2

The Naughty Way: Try this move in a hot tub—you won't regret it. Substitute the bed or chair for the bench in a hot tub and you're good to go.

> "An ingenious person should multiply the kinds
> of congress after the fashion of the different
> kinds of beasts and birds."
>
> —KAMA SUTRA

The Candy Cane

Stand up tall, just like a nice long candy cane, to get the ultimate pleasure from your boinking session. Just try not to break the wall down.

Get into Position:
The man faces the wall and stands tall and rigid as he lifts the woman up. He grabs the back of her thighs and holds her against his hips with her back against the wall. Use the wall for support and leverage as you both thrust with abandon.

Why It Works:
This position is perfect for being up close and personal, and it's also great for a quickie—no bed necessary—when you need a break from all that family time. Just find a closet and have at it.

Difficulty: 3

The Nice Way: You can forgo the lifting and the wall and just go at it in a standing missionary position.

TIP: Try using a real candy cane to add some extra mint and spice to your foreplay session as you work up to this position. You can run the candy cane across each other's lips, suck on it sexily, or put it somewhere super naughty.

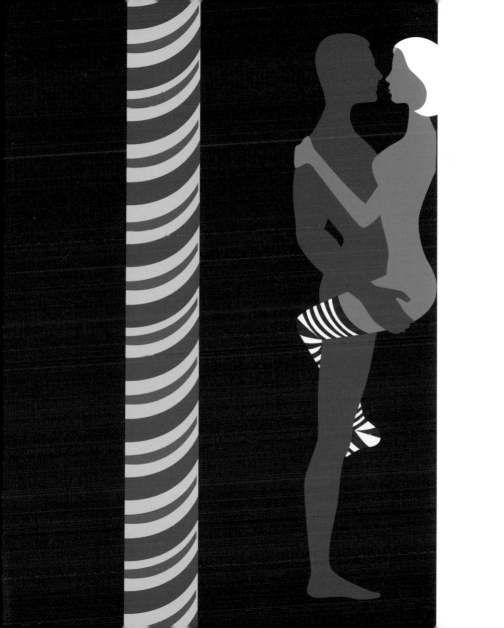

Presents Un
the Tree

Everyone's favorite activity is tearing open the gift-wrappi
plenty of presents to find right under the blankets. Why ru
each other in private?

Get into Position:
The woman lies on her back and lifts her legs over her head so they are parallel to the floor.
If you practice yoga, this should be easy. The man kneels in front of her and presses his knees
against her lower back, supporting her. She can rest her legs on his shoulders. He leans his
torso against her thighs and his hands on the bed to get into a first-class thrusting position.

Why It Works:
Because her legs are up and spread, it allows for extra-deep penetration and lots of luscious rubbing.
And the man feels powerful and in control in this position, so everyone wins. And isn't that the best
gift anyone could ask for?

Difficulty: 4

The Nice Way: If she can't quite get into the folded-over position, she can raise her legs,
bend them at the knee, and leave them in the air, instead of lifting them over her head and
under his shoulders.

The Polar Express

...o take you both to unimagined places as you enjoy a good romp before or ...as dinner. You can do this number in an armless kitchen chair, or take it upstairs ...privacy.

Get into Position:

The guy should sit down on a tall-backed chair and place a pillow behind his lower back for comfort. The gal should hop on his lap and straddle him, with her hands resting behind her on his knees. She should then lean back slightly and lift her legs up (one at a time) so her ankles are resting on his shoulders. Get that train rolling as she begins to thrust back and forth, and then the real party begins.

Why It Works:

The view this position provides is unmatched, so the intimacy and hotness levels instantly skyrocket.

Difficulty: 4

The Nice Way: If the woman can't get her legs up onto the man's shoulders, she can also just squat with her legs resting on the chair, on either side of the man.

Accessories: A tall-backed armless chair and a pillow

Two Turtle Doves

This erotic position will have the two of you reaching new heights together. You'll be as close as Siamese twins as you tense your bodies on top of each other and hold on for the flight.

Get into Position:
The man lies on his back and the woman climbs on top and lowers herself onto his member. Then she elongates and aligns herself with him, limb-to-limb. He should flex his feet so she can use them for leverage as she pumps up and down. Try to keep your bodies tense for maximum satisfaction when you arrive at the big O.

Why It Works:
The friction of your two bodies rubbing against each other will get the fire started, and the rubbing of her clitoris against his pubic bone is bound to please. Plus, the synchronization of your bodies increases the possibility of climaxing simultaneously.

Difficulty: 3

The Nice Way: She can spread her legs into the more classic inverted Mistletoe Mambo (page 11) if she gets tired.

TIP: Hold your arms out to the sides for balance.

Dancer and Prancer

These two reindeer know how to move their hooves, and the two of you will benefit if you master this potent position.

Get into Position:
Face each other and kneel, as you each move one leg outward. The woman then rests her leg on the man's thigh for easy entry. Hold on to each other as you start your bump and grind.

Why It Works:
You two are in prime position for lots of kissing and breast fondling, and your closeness will increase the heat—literally and figuratively.

Difficulty: 3

The Nice Way: Leave your legs where they are when you kneel and just go at it. Spreading both of your legs slightly will give easier access and help with balance.

> "The love of a woman who sees the marks of
> nails on the private parts of her body ...
> becomes again fresh and new."
>
> —KAMA SUTRA

The Bouncing Elf

Get ready for some great bouncy action with this standing number. The man will feel like the hero of Christmas as he carries his elf into climax.

Get into Position:
The man stands and lifts her up from her bottom. She wraps her arms around his shoulders and her legs around his waist. When he enters her, she should hang suspended from him and enjoy the bouncy fun! This position is not for the faint of heart or those who are out of shape, so if you're having trouble, try doing this one the Nice Way.

Why It Works:
This move provides up-and-down action rather than in-and-out, so it should be new and exciting. She will enjoy the pressure on the front of her vaginal wall and he will savor the manly feelings that come from holding up his woman.

Difficulty: 4

The Nice Way: If you find yourselves needing a little support, he can stand with his back to the bed or a sofa and she can rest her feet on it.

TIP: You can easily transition into this pose from Dancing Sugar Plums (page 31). The man should always bend at the knees, keeping his back straight as he lifts her up. Make sure you come out of this position as carefully as you went into it.

Geese A-Goosing

Try not to shake the house down as the two of you get into this sensual pose and start a-playing.

Get into Position:
The man and woman both lie on their sides and scissor their legs together, keeping them bent. Get close and hold on to each other as you bump and grind your way to oblivion.

Why It Works:
You'll be so close to each other the intensity will be magnetic, and you're in prime position for lots of kissing and nibbling. Feel free to let your hands roam around each other's bodies, stroking and scratching in all the right places.

Difficulty: 1

The Naughty Way: She can reach back to stroke her man's testicles while doing Geese A-Goosing, a move we like to call the Nutcracker.

Dancing Sugar Plums

Trust us, you've never seen sugar plums dance like this before. If you like sex standing up but sometimes find it difficult to balance, this dance is for you. No ballet shoes necessary!

Get into Position:
The man and woman stand facing each other, and she lifts up one leg and bends it at the knee. He holds it for support, and it's time to start dancing!

Why It Works:
This move is easy to hold for long periods of time, even though you're standing, so it's perfect for those who don't have a bed handy.

Difficulty: 2

The Nice Way: She can drop her leg and you two can just go at it, in a standing missionary move.

The Naughty Way: If the woman is ballerina-flexible, try the Rockette (page 115): She can lift her leg straight up in the air and rest it against her man's shoulder.

TIP: You can easily transition into the Bouncing Elf (page 27) from this position.

Sliding Down the Chimney

If you'll be playing Santa this year, you might want to get some practice in for squeezing into tight spaces—with your partner, of course. This pose has the two of you gripping each other securely so you're ready to slide through anything!

Get into Position:
The man should kneel down and rest his buttocks on the back of his legs. The woman should climb astride him and wrap her arms and legs around him, holding him in a tight embrace as you move together in a grinding motion.

Why It Works:
This is pretty much as close as you can get, and you'll both enjoy the sweet face-to-face action. The friction created will only heat things up even more.

Difficulty: 1

The Naughty Way: He is in prime position for some nipple-licking action, so have at it!

TIP: You can easily transition into Dancer and Prancer (page 24) from this position.

APHRODISIAC CHRISTMAS TREAT

Sometimes the easiest way to get in the mood is to eat something with aphrodisiac properties, like chocolate, ginger, or oysters. These foods are known to act on the body in special ways, sometimes increasing arousal or even just stimulating blood flow. Try our recipe for Decadent Gingery Hot Cocoa to get you both warmed up and amorous.

Decadent Gingery Hot Cocoa

— Serves 2 —

2 cups milk

½-inch piece peeled, fresh ginger, sliced

4 teaspoons sugar

4 teaspoons unsweetened cocoa powder

4 teaspoons water

Ground ginger

1. In a small saucepan, heat the milk and ginger over medium heat until scalding, about 4 minutes.

2. While the milk is warming, put the sugar and cocoa powder into a bowl.

3. Add the water to the cocoa powder and sugar and stir to make a paste.

4. Remove the ginger from the warmed milk with a slotted spoon.

5. Add the chocolate mixture to the milk and whisk until frothy.

6. Pour the hot chocolate into two mugs.

7. Sprinkle the top with some ground ginger for extra bite.

Now just sit back and enjoy your yummy Christmas treat with your partner before you take it to the bedroom for further indulgence.

CHAPTER 2

Reindeer-Style

now it's time to do it from behind. Although some couples miss the kissing and connection that comes from being face to face, most find that the ultra-deep penetration and G-spot stimulation offered by the rear-entry angle more than make up for it. While the kids are downstairs opening presents, the parents can give each other their gifts of dual orgasms in the bedroom. These positions are top-notch for intense climaxing and you'll certainly have a blast behaving like animals! Try Reindeers Gone Wild and Roasted Chestnuts if you're a first-timer, and move on from there to the Hanging Ornament, the Downhill Toboggan, and the Snowmobile. Remember to hold on tight!

Reindeers Gone Wild

This classic position will have the two of you going at it like, well, animals. Try putting on some antler headbands for added Christmas cheer. Go buck wild!

Get into Position:
The lady gets down on all fours, and the gent kneels behind her with his legs together, grabbing onto her sides as he enters her from behind.

Why It Works:
While this position lacks face-to-face contact, it makes up for it with the intense thrusting action that hits the woman in all the right places. It's also easy for the man to reach around her body and stimulate her clitoris as an added bonus.

Difficulty: 2

The Naughty Way: She closes her legs and he gets into a crouching position, giving him more thrusting power and leverage.

Accessories: Antler headbands

The Hanging Ornament

In this case, the ornament is the woman! This standing position gives him access from behind as she bends over and waits to be hung on his tree.

Get into Position:
The woman bends over at the waist and rests her hands on the floor or holds onto her ankles. He enters from behind and holds onto her waist as he begins thrusting.

Why It Works:
This maneuver is perfect for those times when you can't lie down or only have time for a frenzied quickie—like in between dinner and dessert or during the annual but boring secret Santa exchange. There's also plenty of opportunity for the man's hands to wander from breasts to clitoris and back.

Difficulty: 3

The Nice Way: She leans forward with a flat back and rests her hands on her knees or on a chair or other sturdy surface.

TIP: She can spread her legs apart for some variation.

Roasted Chestnu'

This position is so hot you'll be able to roast anything within a five-f͏ variation on the standard rear-entry pose and you'll both be all hot ͏

Get into Position:
One way to get into this position is to start out in the Reindeers Gone Wild position (page ͏ and then lift your torsos so you are both upright and kneeling. Alternatively, you can just start ͏ kneeling, with the man behind the woman.

Why It Works:
This pose allows for a lot of rubbing between your bodies, and the man's hands are also free to caress the woman's breasts and stimulate her clitorally. That will really get her chestnuts roasting!

Difficulty: 2

The Nice Way: You can do this position standing upright as well; it's a little tamer because it's more difficult to thrust as hard from a standing position. If the lady is a lot shorter, she can stand on a stair or stool, or just put on some heels.

TIP: She might want to lean on a wall or bedpost for balance, or she can hold onto his butt to stay upright.

Star Atop the Tree

s partner pleaser, the woman lies facedown with her arms and legs spread out, resembling ar. And as soon as the man climbs on board, you can bet she will light up.

Get into Position:
The woman lies facedown with her legs open and slightly bent at the knee. Her arms are spread out to either side for balance and her bottom should be pushed up into the air. The man enters from behind, with his legs together and arms on either side, similar to a relaxed push-up position.

Why It Works:
This pose gives easy access to the man and also allows for close, intimate contact, even though the two of you aren't facing each other. It's also easy for the woman to pleasure herself while the man is thrusting away.

Difficulty: 3

The Naughty Way: The woman can close her legs while the man puts his on the outside, bent at the knee, in a more riding-friendly pose. This provides thrilling G-spot stimulation for the woman.

TIP: You can place a small pillow underneath the woman's pelvis to help raise her bottom and make entry even easier.

Naughty Mrs. Claus

Mrs. Claus isn't all cookies and milk all the time, you know. This nasty number has her on all fours as Santa takes charge from behind.

Get into Position:
The woman gets down on all fours on a bed or couch, while the man stands behind her and holds onto her hips as he pumps in and out.

Why It Works:
This pose is great for G-spot stimulation and also allows the woman to rub her clitoris simultaneously. It also gives the man control of the angle and pumping pace, which he is sure to enjoy.

Difficulty: 3

The Naughty Way: For even more depravity, the woman can kneel on the floor with her chest draped over the bed while he squats behind her.

The Downhill Toboggan

You'll feel like you're rocketing down a snow-covered hill when you start this sexy session. While it's a bit tricky to get into this pose, once you're in it you're sure to enjoy the ensuing adventure.

Get into Position:
The guy sits up straight with his legs extended in front of him on the bed. The gal faces away from him and straddles his waist, extending her legs back so they are nearly behind him, with her stomach and chest on the bed between his feet. Her arms wrap around his feet, providing leverage as she slides up and down, creating lots of friction.

Why It Works:
You'll both be proud of yourselves for getting into this pose, and she will love the control she has over the speed and depth of the thrust, while her partner can just enjoy the ride—and view.

Difficulty: 5

The Naughty Way: Try putting this pose on an incline by having the man sit on some pillows for even deeper penetration.

"As regards kissing, a wager may be laid
as to which will get hold of the lips
of the other first."

—KAMA SUTRA

The Snowmobile

Get strapped in and ready to ride this sizzling snowmobile all the way to O-town. You definitely need to be flexible to handle this machine, but it's worth it!

Get into Position:
The man lies down on his back. The woman straddles him facing his feet. She then arches her back and lies down backwards on top of him, giving him open access to her breasts and clitoris for maximum satisfaction.

Why It Works:
As mentioned above, the man has an easy approach to clitoral and nipple stimulation, so both partners should be on their way to ecstasy quickly.

Difficulty: 5

The Naughty Way: Get super bonus points for actually doing this outside in the snow!

TIP: The woman should limber up beforehand with some simple stretches so she doesn't injure herself getting in and out of this position.

Accessories: Ski goggles and scarves

Santa's Lap

Whether you were good or bad this year, this position will have both of you getting an exciting present. Just tell Santa what you want and hope he's as naughty as you are.

Get into Position:
The man sits down on the edge of the bed or chair and the woman lowers herself onto his lap, facing away from him. The man can plant his feet on the floor for more thrusting power.

Why It Works:
The kink factor is pretty high, especially if the two of you take your roles seriously. The woman can also use her hand to stimulate the man's testicles or perineum, in a move we call the Nutcracker.

Difficulty: 2

The Naughty Way: For deeper penetration, the woman can bring her knees up to her chest, with her feet on the edge of the bed or chair.

Accessories: Santa hat and beard

Elves in Santa's Workshop

What do you think Santa's elves do when they take a break from toy-making? Perhaps they try their hands at lovemaking, with this raunchy maneuver that will excite and satisfy both partners.

Get into Position:
The woman straddles her legs over an armless chair and holds onto the back of it. Her partner squats on the edge of the chair behind her and begins thrusting.

Why It Works:
Although he will get quite a workout (but think of how amazing his quads will feel!), he will also get a lot of pleasure from this innovative rear-entry move. The woman will get prime G-spot stimulation, which is all any woman wants for Christmas anyway, right?

Difficulty: 5

The Nice Way: If you don't have a suitable chair, move over to the edge of the bed where you can both squat down on the floor, while she holds on to the bed for balance.

TIP: Make sure you use a stable chair and hold on tight so you don't tip over in all the excitement!

Accessories: Armless chair

The North Pole

You two will need to keep warm this winter somehow, and everyone knows body heat is the best way to do that. So snuggle up and spoon each other tenderly as you relish this romantic posture.

Get into Position:
Both partners lie on their sides, with the man molding his body to the woman's as she faces away from him. Get cozy and hold each other tight as the man gently pushes into her from behind.

Why It Works:
This position is perfect for when romance strikes and you just want to be close to each other. It's also easy for the man to massage the woman's breasts and clitoris from this angle.

Difficulty: 2

The Naughty Way: For a nastier way to spoon, he lies on his back and the woman gets on top, but with her back resting on his chest. She bends her knees and he grabs hold of her chest as he begins to thrust. It's not quite as romantic, but it provides the same kind of chest-to-back closeness.

TIP: Try this move on a blanket in front of the fireplace for ultimate coziness.

A CHRISTMAS STRIPTEASE

A striptease is a great way to get yourselves in the mood before making love, and either partner can be the stripper. What better gift is there than unwrapping yourself in front of your partner? Whether you're a first timer or an old pro, try these tips to make your performance seasonally appropriate but still super sexy:

* Get into the holiday spirit by transforming yourself into a nympho-elf, Santa's Hot Little Helper, or a sexy Santa or Mrs. Claus. Lots of costume stores and websites sell sexy Christmas outfits like these. You can also tie yourself up in big red velvet ribbons, or you can just wrap yourself in lights and slowly unravel them.

* Play some Christmas music in the background, as you'll need something you can dance to—but stay away from anything too religious. Some great options are "All I Want for Christmas Is You" by Mariah Carey and "Santa Baby" by Kylie Minogue.

* Suck on a candy cane during your performance or do something naughty with an ornament or some eggnog. The possibilities are endless!

"By union with men
the lust, desire, or
passion of women
is satisfied."

—Kama Sutra

CHAPTER 3

Open Sleigh

What better way to show your love on Christmas than by giving your partner multiple bed-rocking orgasms? These lady's-legs-up positions are as hot as they come—allowing for ultra-deep penetration and access to that elusive yet bliss-inducing G-spot. Try the Manger for up-close face-to-face intimacy, Stoking the Fire if you're feeling energized (and flexible!) pre- or post-Christmas dinner, or O Christmas Tree for some slow, sensuous nookie.

Santa and His Sleigh

You and your partner will enjoy playing Santa and sleigh in this ultra-pleasurable position. Just like the big man, the person on top takes the reins and leads the treasure-filled sleigh into the night.

Get into Position:
The woman lies on her back on the edge of a bed, couch, coffee table, or sleigh (if it's Christmas Eve), with feet flat on the floor. He kneels or stands beside the edge of the surface, between his partner's legs, with hands holding her hips to add oomph to the thrust. For optimal angling, find a surface that's about one foot lower than the height of the man's pelvis.

Why It Works:
Not only is Santa's sleigh a comfortable ride for both partners, with a little upward tilt of the woman's pelvis, it also allows for deep penetration, G-spot access, and lots of feel-good friction.

Super-sexy bonus: This sleigh gives Santa lots of freedom to move, so he can really take the reins in varying the pace and direction of his thrusts. There's also plenty of opportunity for clitoral stimulation—either partner can use a free hand to enhance the ride.

Difficulty: 1

The Naughty Way: For a more intense sleigh ride, the woman can lift her legs straight up to rest atop her man's shoulders. This allows for a deeper thrust and a quicker route to Christmas joy (unless this Santa is too big for the ride).

The Nice Way: The woman can sit up on the edge of the bed and hold onto her man's shoulders. This lessens the intensity but increases the intimacy quotient with opportunities for prolonged eye contact and kissing.

The Manger

This manger is **nothing** *like the one you're used to seeing during the holidays—and thank goodness for that.*

Get into Position:
With the man kneeling on the bed, the woman straddles his lap, plants her feet on either side, and leans back on her hands to support her upper body.

Why It Works:
This close face-to-face position is sensual and vigorous, as it allows for intimate eye contact, small, tight grinding movements, and a great frontal view for the man.

Difficulty: 2

The Naughty Way: For a more athletic variation (and to hit different pleasure spots), transition into Stoking the Fire (page 67): He lifts himself to his knees, also lifting his partner's lower torso with him. She arches her back to align her pelvis with his, plants her feet, and leaves her upper back and shoulders resting on the bed.

Stoking the Fire

When the weather outside is frightful, turn the heat up with some rea
Who needs a fireplace when you can get sweaty with this sizzling move?

Get into Position:
The woman lies flat on her back, while her partner kneels between her legs. She plants her feet and arches her back to align her pelvis with his, forming a half-bridge, with upper back resting on the bed to support this extreme angle.

Why It Works:
The almost upside-down positioning allows for deep penetration and yields a great thigh workout for both partners. He can either hold her hips from underneath to offer support or use one hand on her easily reached lady parts. She can prop her back and shoulders with a pillow to prevent any neck discomfort.

Difficulty: 4

The Naughty Way: For an extra athletic challenge, the woman can alter the angle of penetration by lifting her upper body off the bed with her arms, forming a full bridge.

The Yule Log

*Yule Log might not burn for long, but it **will** create some dazzling sparks.*

Get into Position:
With him kneeling, she lies flat on her back with her legs straight up and resting on his shoulders.

Why It Works:
When pelvises align comfortably, the angle created allows for deep, exhilarating penetration. Use pillows if it's necessary to adjust heights. The woman can use her free hands to stimulate her clitoris or his testicles, and the man will enjoy this power position and the lively scenic view.

Difficulty: 2

The Nice Way: To make this easier, the woman can drop one leg and wrap it around her partner's knee.

The Nicer Way: To make it even easier (it *is* the holidays after all), move to the edge of the bed (or couch) so the man can stand and align his pelvis with hers.

The Naughty Way: For a tighter squeeze and super-hot friction, the woman can straighten her legs and hold them as high as she can, while her partner holds them a bit to the side. This tilts her position slightly, offering a new breathtaking angle of penetration.

Elf Action

Elves can be sexy too. This curled-up position allows for powerful penetration—all you'll need is a little elf hat to complete the trick.

Get into Position:
With the woman curled up on her back with knees to her chest, the man kneels by her backside with hands on her hips or thighs. The thrusting, bouncing, and swaying motions will raise her hips with every beat. Place a pillow beneath her hips for extra leverage.

Why It Works:
This variation on the Yule Log (page 68) intensifies G-spot stimulation and allows for deep penetration.

Difficulty: 1

The Naughty Way: To modify Elf Action, she can easily change her leg positions for different sensations: feet planted on his chest, knees spread, or flung over his shoulders (see the Yule Log, page 68).

Accessories: Pillow and an elf hat

Reindeer Games

On Donner, on Blitzen! Santa's reindeer never had as much fun as you will with this acrobatic move. The lady might need to do some leg stretches beforehand to work on flexibility, but the sensations are well worth it.

Get into Position:
The woman lies on her side, with her top leg extended straight up or resting on her partner's opposite shoulder, and her bottom leg between his legs on the bed. She can support her head with her bottom arm, as shown.

Why It Works:
This is another great move for extra-deep penetration, and the woman can experiment with her positioning by wriggling or twisting her body to find new sweet spots.

Difficulty: 3

The Nice Way: If this proves uncomfortable, or if her extended leg begins to tire, she should bend it at the knee and rest her shin on her partner's chest, or curl her leg around his backside.

Ebenezer Screw

This sexy twisted move can turn even the crabbiest Scrooge into a stud [...] get into the Screw, those "Bah, humbug"s will become "Oh, yes Ebenez[...]

Get into Position:
With the man kneeling beside the bed, she curls up, knees to chest, and lies on her side at the edge of the bed.

Why It Works:
This twisted position offers a sexy sideways angle and plenty of freedom to move for the guy. For the lady, it offers titillatingly deep penetration.

Difficulty: 1

The Naughty Way: For even more intensity, the woman can pull her legs up closer to her chest.

> "Women being of a tender nature,
> want tender beginnings."
>
> —KAMA SUTRA

Merry Merry X-Mas

Put the X back in X-Mas by trying this easy crossed-leg move.

Get into Position:
The woman lies flat on her back, with her knees curled toward her chest and ankles crossed into an X. The man kneels with legs closed and places her rear end on his lap. She keeps her thighs closed tight and rests her feet on his chest when he begins thrusting. Her hands are free to clutch, massage, and stroke his thighs, while he can grab hold of her hips or thighs for momentum.

Why It Works:
This otherwise basic move gets a merry, merry upgrade with the lady's crossed legs: The tight X makes for extra friction, which you'll both appreciate.

Difficulty: 1

Bonus Move: The woman's curled-up position is perfect for working those PC muscles, which tighten the area around his penis and stimulate her pleasure zones.

The Nice Way: If her legs start to cramp up from the tight curl, she can uncross them and assume the Elf Action position (page 71) or fling them over his shoulders to transition into the Yule Log (page 68).

O Christmas Tree

*This is a tree that should **not** leave the bedroom—and trust us, you won't want to leave your bedroom anyway. Just try not to belt out "O Christmas Tree, O Christmas Tree" while in action.*

Get into Position:

The woman lies on her back missionary-style, with arms extended to her sides and feet planted on the bed. Her man lies beneath her bent legs, perpendicular to her body, with his lower torso turned toward her, ready for action.

Why It Works:

This sideways position offers a different angle from the usual man-on-top moves. Because of the unusual angle, movements will be slow and sensual rather than fast and forceful. You'll hit brand-new spots and the man will get a superior view of the action.

Difficulty: 1

The Naughty Way: If you are willing to sacrifice face time for a new angle, you can transition into the Sizzlin' Snowflake (page 112): The woman turns to her side so her back is facing her partner, and then places her bottom leg between his so your legs are interlocked in a scissor position.

Accessories: She can wrap herself in tinsel for this sexy tree lighting.

TWELVE DAYS OF SEXMAS

On the first day of Christmas,
My true love gave to me
An orgasm that sent me to my knees

On the second day of Christmas,
My true love gave to me
Two bitten nipples,
And an orgasm that sent me to my knees

On the third day of Christmas,
My true love gave to me
Three long licks,
Two bitten nipples,
And an orgasm that sent me to my knees

On the fourth day of Christmas,
My true love gave to me
Four steamy breaths,
Three long licks,
Two bitten nipples,
And an orgasm that sent me to my knees

On the fifth day of Christmas,
My true love gave to me
Five tongue-filled kisses,
Four steamy breaths,
Three long licks,
Two bitten nipples,
And an orgasm that sent me to my knees

On the sixth day of Christmas,
My true love gave to me
Six sultry spanks,
Five tongue-filled kisses,
Four steamy breaths,
Three long licks,
Two bitten nipples,
And an orgasm that sent me to my knees

On the seventh day of Christmas,
My true love gave to me
Seven dirty words,
Six sultry spanks,
Five tongue-filled kisses,
Four steamy breaths,
Three long licks,
Two bitten nipples,
And an orgasm that sent me to my knees

On the **eighth** day of Christmas,
My true love gave to me
Eight naughty nibbles,
Seven dirty words,
Six sultry spanks,
Five tongue-filled kisses,
Four steamy breaths,
Three long licks,
Two bitten nipples,
And an orgasm that sent me to my knees

On the **ninth** day of Christmas,
My true love gave to me
Nine tender touches,
Eight naughty nibbles,
Seven dirty words,
Six sultry spanks,
Five tongue-filled kisses,
Four steamy breaths,
Three long licks,
Two bitten nipples,
And an orgasm that sent me to my knees

On the **tenth** day of Christmas,
My true love gave to me
Ten sucked toes,
Nine tender touches,
Eight naughty nibbles,
Seven dirty words,
Six sultry spanks,
Five tongue-filled kisses,
Four steamy breaths,
Three long licks,
Two bitten nipples,
And an orgasm that sent me to my knees

On the **eleventh** day of Christmas,
My true love gave to me
Eleven tingling tickles,
Ten sucked toes,
Nine tender touches,
Eight naughty nibbles,
Seven dirty words,
Six sultry spanks,
Five tongue-filled kisses,
Four steamy breaths,
Three long licks,
Two bitten nipples,
And an orgasm that sent me to my knees

On the **twelfth** day of Christmas,
My true love gave to me
Twelve sensual strokes,
Eleven tingling tickles,
Ten sucked toes,
Nine tender touches,
Eight naughty nibbles,
Seven dirty words,
Six sultry spanks,
Five tongue-filled kisses,
Four steamy breaths,
Three long licks,
Two bitten nipples,
And an orgasm that sent me to my knees

JINGLE BALLS

Looking for some ways to introduce more Christmas cheer into your shagging session? Here are a few suggestions for increasing the holiday joy:

* Cover his member in red or green frosting (or do stripes if you're really artistic!) and then she can spend lots of time licking it all off.

* Dip his testicles into a glass of eggnog and then she slurps it off, using her tongue to tickle him.

* Attach some bells to a cock ring and slip it on him before coitus; feel the merriness increase as the bells jingle in time with your thrusting action.

CHAPTER 4

Reindeer Riding

The lady is at the reins in this chapter—on top! These steamy moves are for the woman who likes to be in control and for the man who loves watching his lady get hot-and-bothered while getting off. For beginners, start with the tame Rudolph's Ride or the Santa Bounce. To stimulate different pleasure zones, reverse the riding position with Rudolph in Reverse and the Ho-Ho-Hop, which forgo clitoral action to focus on the G-spot. For double-whammy orgasm potential, give the Rocking Horse Romp a try. And if the rider is limber and adventurous, experiment with moves like the Elf Bop, the Luge, and Rockin' Around the Christmas Tree. With all the variety of positions in this chapter, your holiday season is sure to be quite a ride!

Rudolph's Ride

If only Rudolph and his crew could be so lucky to enjoy this timeless, super-sexy move. More commonly known as Cowgirl, the basic woman-on-top position is one of the best-loved in every couple's repertoire.

Get into Position:
With the man flat on his back, the woman straddles him on her knees and supports herself with her arms on his chest or on the bed.

Why It Works:
This position is a classic for good reason: The woman on top holds the reins and controls the pace, angle, and depth of penetration, while the guy on bottom gets a full-frontal view of the sexy scenery.

Difficulty: 2

The Naughty Way: Leaning back and resting her hands on her man's thighs provides a nice push-off for the lady, and an even greater view from below.

The Nice Way: To transition into Silent Night (page 12), an up-close, intimate position—the woman can lean forward and rest her hands on the bed above his shoulders.

Rudolph in Reverse

Riding in reverse might not be advisable for a reindeer (yes, even Rudolph), but for a hot and steamy couple, it'll knock your stockings off.

Get into Position:
The man lies flat on his back while the woman straddles him facing his feet, with her knees on either side of him. She can support herself by resting her hands on his legs or on the bed. Or she can lean back and place her hands on his sides.

Why It Works:
This reverse woman-on-top position offers great opportunity for G-spot stimulation and, like Rudolph's Ride (page 89), it puts the woman in charge of pace, angle, and depth of penetration. She can vary her movements easily: up and down, back and forth, or in circles. Plus, guys enjoy Rudolph in Reverse for the sexy rear-end view.

Difficulty: 2

The Naughty Way: Take this Ride up a notch by transitioning into the Snowmobile (page 51): The woman lies back completely on top of her Rudolph. This acrobatic move will require a little flexibility on her part, but it also gives the man ample opportunity for touching and stroking.

The Maid
A-Milking

You'll be leaping for Christmas joy when you try this energetic variation on Rudolph's Ride.
Bonus: *The maid will get a great leg workout!*

Get into Position:
The man lies flat on his back, while the woman straddles him with her feet planted on the bed and her hands resting on his chest or shoulders or on the bed for support. He can support her squat by placing his hands beneath her thighs or rear end.

Why It Works:
By modifying the on-top position from kneeling to squatting, the woman allows for even deeper penetration. This rodeo-style move gives the woman control over the speed, depth, and angle of movements.

Difficulty: 3

The Naughty Way: The woman can rotate to the reverse Maid A-Milking position so she's facing her partner's feet. This modification hits different sweet spots—instead of clitoral stimulation, she'll be prime for G-spot action, and he'll enjoy the view from behind.

Rockin' Around the Christmas Tree

Every great holiday party should end with some rockin' around the tree, and this athletic move is a party of its own. Have some Christmas cookies—and water—on hand to replenish your energy before, during, and after.

Get into Position:
The man sits up with legs extended in front of him, while his lady sits on his lap facing him and leans back so her legs rest over his shoulders and her arms support her from behind.

Why It Works:
Although this move is quite vigorous, and it can be difficult to find and keep a rhythm, the rewards are rockin'. The woman's got control over the angle of penetration and does most of the thrusting and bouncing, while the gent can bounce up to help her out. This one relies on the strength of her arms and the action in her hips, so a little toning up beforehand will help get you both to blissful heights.

Difficulty: 5

The Nice Way: To make this easier (but equally as rockin'), transition into the Santa Bounce (page 97): The woman plants her feet on the bed behind her partner, rather than resting them on his shoulders. This gives her more freedom to move and greater balance, and both partners can thrust in equal measure.

The Santa Bounce

After a gut-busting holiday dinner, you and your partner will need an intimate evening of close face time and tender action. This low-key version of Rockin' Around the Christmas Tree (page 94) is perfect for post-party playtime.

Get into Position:
With the man sitting straight up and his legs extended in front of him, the woman straddles his lap with feet planted on the bed at his sides and arms grabbing his shoulders for close-contact support.

Why It Works:
This highly passionate move ups the intimacy quotient, making things ultra steamy without all the acrobatics required of its more extreme counterpart. The subtle rocking and bouncing motions and close face-to-face positioning give you ample opportunity for kissing and touching, and the guy can assist with the grinding motions by moving his partner around from beneath her bum.

Difficulty: 2

The Nice Way: For more bouncing action and a tighter grip, the woman can hold onto her partner's thighs while he hugs her close.

Accessories: Santa hat and beard

The Luge

This downhill ride offers maximum thrills for ladies who are particularly bendy. You might want to stretch out your torso and thighs before mounting this racy toboggan.

Get into Position:
The man lies flat on his back, while the woman straddles him, with knees planted on the bed on either side of him. She leans back and rests her upper body and arms on the lower half of his legs, as shown.

Why It Works:
This angle is incredibly stimulating for the woman, offering her partner total access to her lady parts.

Difficulty: 4

The Nice Way: If this stretch is uncomfortable for the lady, she can sit up into Rudolph's Ride (page 89) for a less strenuous position.

"The embrace which indicated the mutual love ... is of four kinds: Touching, Piercing, Rubbing, Pressing."

—KAMA SUTRA

Rocking Horse Romp

*This frisky woman-on-top move is one exhilarating ride—much more so tha[n]
you got for Christmas as a kid.*

Get into Position:
The man lies flat on his back with one leg extended and one knee bent. Facing his feet, his partner straddles his bent leg, with her knees planted on the bed on either side of It. She lowers herself onto him, and leans forward against his leg.

Why It Works:
The Romp focuses on several of the lady's pleasure zones: The friction created by rocking against her man's leg stimulates her clitoris, while the up-and-down thrusting and circle motions work wonders on the walls of her vagina. She controls the pace and depth of penetration, and he gets a prime view of her backside.

Difficulty: 2

The Nice Way: If she gets tired, she can lie back onto her partner's chest and transition into the Snowmobile (page 51).

Accessories: Cowboy hat

TIP: The cowgirl can make him neigh by rubbing or scratching his thigh during the ride.

The Ho-Ho-Hop

Santa will go wild when you tell him everything you want for Christmas this year. You can bring this kneeling position anywhere—the couch, a kitchen chair, the stairs—for all-purpose action.

Get into Position:
With the man seated on the edge of the bed, or on a couch or chair, and his legs close together, his partner straddles him facing away and kneels.

Why It Works:
The Ho-Ho-Hop offers the woman deep penetration and total control over speed, depth, and angle of penetration. Her partner's hands are free to roam from her hips to her chest to her lady parts.

Difficulty: 2

The Naughty Way: If her thighs can take it, she can plant her feet on the floor into an almost-standing position between his legs.

TIP: Stick a pillow under her knees to relieve any strain on her thighs.

Candy Cane Cowgirl

Don't try this move after Christmas dinner—unless you're ready for a workout with a belly full of ham. This woman-on-top variation of the Maid A-Milking (page 93) is tough on the knees but oh-so-good, thanks to the unusual angle.

Get into Position:
With the man lying flat on his back, the woman mounts him from the side, feet planted on the bed. She can lean back to support herself with her hands on the bed.

Why It Works:
The unique positioning offers new sideways sensations for both partners.

Difficulty: 4

The Nice Way: For a slightly easier variation, the man should lie on his back on a couch or low bed, while the woman stands and lowers herself down on top.

TIP: You can easily transition into O Christmas Tree (page 79), with the lady lying back completely with her knees up, and her partner turning to his side and thrusting from a perpendicular position.

The Elf Bop

Who knew elves could have this much fun? (And who knew they were so flexible?)

Get into Position:
The man lies flat on his back with his knees curled toward his chest, while the woman straddles him from under his thighs with her feet planted on the bed. The man can offer support by holding her rear end or upper thighs.

Why It Works:
This unique angle puts the woman in the ultimate power position, and she can bounce and thrust at her own pace while controlling depth. Since the range of thrust movement is short and shallow, the Elf Bop stimulates the supersensitive tip of his penis and the outer regions of her vagina. The face-to-face positioning allows for steamy eye contact and, if she's got good balance, there's plenty of opportunity for fondling his elf parts.

Difficulty: 5

The Nice Way: If the squatting gets tiresome for the lady, she can kneel with her legs straddling her partner's rear end.

The Naughty Way: If you're both up for an elfish adventure, reverse this move so the woman is facing her partner's feet and resting on the backs of his legs. She can mount him either squatting or kneeling.

CHAPTER 5

Reckless
XXX-Mas

Finally, here's good ol' holiday fun for the truly adventurous. Some moves in this chapter call for acrobatic flair, such as the Stocking Stuffer, the Rockette, and Lord A-Leaping, while others are just difficult to get into, such as the Sizzlin' Snowflake, St. Nick's Twist, and the Inverted Unholy Cross. These positions require experience, patience, and skill (not to mention courage!). But once you get the hang of them, your Christmas spirit will shoot through the chimney.

Stocking Stuffer

After you hang your stockings on the fireplace, get ready for the ultimate bag o' tricks. This move requires extreme agility and patience, but the gifts are well worth the exceptional physicality.

Get Into Position:

To start, the woman lies flat on her back and then lifts her lower body with her hands planted on the ground for support. She lifts her rear end and legs straight up to the sky until she reaches a shoulder stand, while her partner kneels at her back and assists by holding her legs and placing his body against hers. She rests her legs on his shoulders and grabs his thighs for support. He grabs onto her hips and aligns their bodies to get ready for action.

Why It Works:

The upside-down positioning unleashes an exhilarating blood rush from the woman's legs to her loins, resulting in powerful, unique sensations. Her legs are straight and close together, giving him a snug, sexy fit.

Difficulty: 5

The Nice Way: If the shoulder stand proves too challenging, move the Stuffer over to the edge of the bed, so the woman can lie on her back with her legs up while her partner stands facing her on the floor, next to the edge.

TIP: During the action, the woman can squeeze her legs together to enhance her partner's sensations.

The Sizzlin' Snowflake

Every snowflake is beautiful and unique... especially when it's in the sack. This position gets its name from the six-pointed shape created by the couple's bodies. It might look complicated, but when you get it right, this snowflake is sizzling.

Get into Position:
The man lies on his side with his legs spread, while the woman lies on her side facing away from him and perpendicular to his body. They interlock their legs into a scissor position: his leg on bottom, then hers, then his, then hers.

Why It Works:
Although the Sizzlin' Snowflake doesn't require acrobatics or high-octane intensity, it still creates fireworks thanks to the unusual angle of penetration. The movements are slow and tender, creating an intimate experience even though there's limited eye contact.

Difficulty: 4

The Nice Way: To make this move more intimate and controlled, the man can sit up and hold his partner's hip and rear end, while she props herself up on her side. Their open, scissored legs will close up a bit, resulting in greater friction.

The Rockette

This Christmas Spectacular definitely requires some warm-up high kicks before attempting. But for the flexible female, this primo move is titillating fun.

Get into Position:
The couple stands facing one another, while the woman lifts one leg so it rests on her partner's shoulder. He supports this precarious stance by grasping at her knee and around her waist.

Why It Works:
The face-to-face contact adds an intimate touch to this otherwise not-so-cozy standing position, while her outstretched leg offers a snug squeeze for penetration.

Difficulty: 5

The Nice Way: If she's not a prima ballerina in the flexibility department, she can wrap her extended leg around his hip for more support, transitioning into Dancing Sugar Plums (page 31). You can also stand against a wall for better balance.

"Whatever things may be done
by one of the lovers to the other,
the same should be returned."

—KAMA SUTRA

Comet's Big Dip

Reindeer games don't get any more exhilarating than in this ultra-hot holiday move.

Get into Position:
With the man sitting on the edge of a bed or couch, his partner straddles his lap, facing him, then leans back so the top of her body hangs off the edge. He supports her by grasping onto her hips and hands.

Why It Works:
This position can be thrilling for the suspended lady, who enjoys the unique angle, deep penetration, and G-spot access, as well as the excitement of dangling off a ledge while her partner has total control of her body. He gets to take the ultimate power position and is able to savor the full-frontal view.

Difficulty: 4

The Nice Way: To avoid back strain on the lady, she can sit straight up on her partner's lap, which also allows for steamy eye contact.

TIP: Instead of holding onto her partner, she can reach her hands over her head to support herself using the floor.

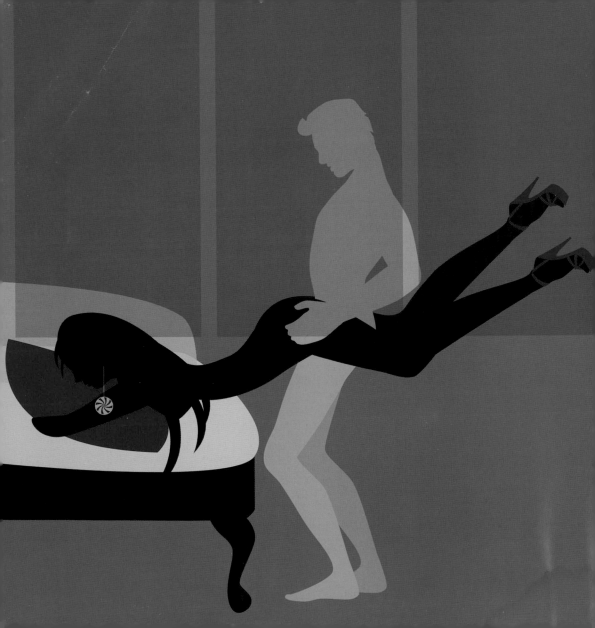

Lord A-Leaping

You and your lover will feel like you're flying through the air when you try this thrillingly risky move.

Get into Position:
Stand in front of a couch, bed, or other firm surface with the woman close to the edge and the man standing behind her. She places her hands on the surface in front of her, while he lifts her by the thighs—feet and all!—and aligns himself for penetration. He holds her securely at her hips and lower waist, while she keeps her abdomen tight to sustain the leaping position.

Why It Works:
This acrobatic rear-entry move allows for fantastic, deep penetration, and it puts the gent in total control of his partner's body.

Difficulty: 5

The Nice Way: Take the height (and strain on the lady's upper body) down a notch by bringing the Lord A-Leaping to the floor: She can support herself using her arms and abdomen, rather than just wrists and hands, and he can kneel for the action.

St. Nick's Twist

The North Pole trembles when Mr. and Mrs. Claus maneuver themselves into this twisted sideways position.

Get into Position:
The woman lies on her side with hands extended above her head, while the man positions himself between her legs, also on his side, and perpendicular to her. Once both are in position, he holds onto her shoulders and she holds steady by keeping her hands stretched out in front of her.

Why It Works:
The unique sideways positioning explores new angles and sweet spots for both partners, particularly the side walls of her vagina. Plus, you'll have freedom to vary the style of penetration—from deep thrusts to short grinding motions. The woman can twist her hips slightly to find angles that drive you both wild.

Difficulty: 4

The Naughty Way: To turn this into a power move, the man can kneel and the woman can lift her top leg so her calf rests on his shoulder. He should straddle her bottom thigh and hug her top thigh before getting down to business.

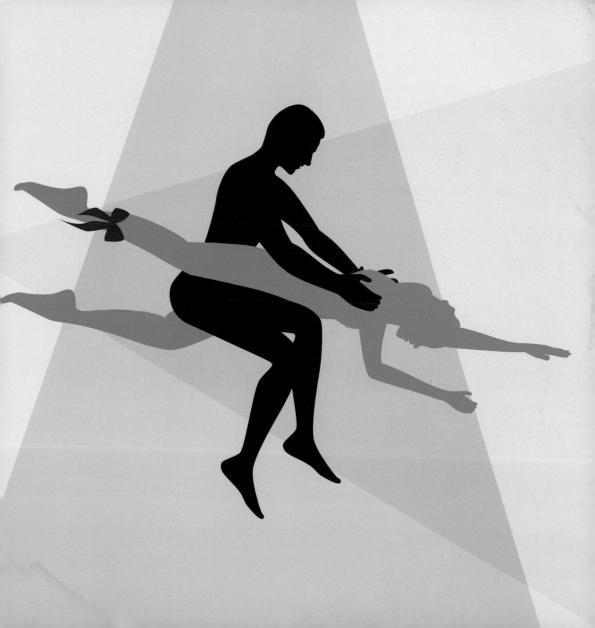

French Hens

Hens flexible enough to achieve this position find it to be an incredib

Get into Position:
The man sits up on the bed with legs straight out in front of him, while his p~
She bends backward so her head rests between his legs, and raises her arms to grab no..
for support and momentum. He can wrap his arms around her waist or hold on tightly at her hips.

Why It Works:
The backward bend and close squeeze create a deeply sensual connection. With her head back and arms behind her, the lady feels completely surrendered to the ecstasy of the move, while her man gets a sexy, unobstructed view of her body.

Difficulty: 4

The Nice Way: If the backbend starts to be a strain, she can sit up straight into the Ho-Ho-Hop (page 102).

TIP: The man can lean forward and pull her up while thrusting for a super-scintillating hug.

The Inverted Unholy Cross

Leave the holiday's holiness outside when attempting this raunchy Cross-shaped move.

Get into Position:
The man sits straight up with his legs spread, while his partner lies on her back with legs resting on his shoulders.

Why It Works:
Although mobility is limited because of the guy's seated position, the Cross offers ultra-deep penetration and opportunity for plenty of lusty eye contact and stroking.

Difficulty: 3

The Naughty Way: To transition into the more active Yule Log position (page 68), he can bring himself to a kneel for stronger thrusting power.

TIP: This move puts the lady in prime position to receive some oral stimulation if she raises her hips up from the bed and wraps her legs around his neck.

Christmas Banquet

'Tis the season to give... and to receive. If you're both fans of giving and receiving oral stimulation, save room for this feast during the holiday season. Arguably the most popular oral sextivity, the 69 position offers both partners simultaneous pleasure—the man performs cunnilingus on his woman, and she performs fellatio on her man. Just remember to keep up the good work while your partner is digging in.

Get into Position:
The man lies flat on his back, while the woman straddles his face and places her face in position above his genitals. You lick, suck, and kiss one another's sweet spots, either as mouth-watering foreplay or the lip-smacking entrée.

Why It Works:
The dual oral stimulation is an ultra-intimate way to pleasure one another at the same time. Giving while receiving increases the heat for people who relish in feeling their partner's excitement—and this position holds you close enough to feel every shiver, shake, and tremble.

Difficulty: 3

The Nice Way: Make this a little more comfortable by lying on your sides, each with your top leg bent at the knee and foot planted on the bed. This way, you can rest your heads on one another's bottom thighs. The sideways Christmas Banquet is great for endurance if you two want to take your sweet time.

TIP: If you're unable to focus on your own enjoyment while performing on your partner, take care of business one person at a time. Or don't worry so much about climaxing and simply enjoy this fun, sexy position as foreplay.

About Cider Mill Press
Book Publishers

Good ideas ripen with time. From seed to harvest, Cider Mill Press brings fine reading, information, and entertainment together between the covers of its creatively crafted books. Our Cider Mill bears fruit twice a year, publishing a new crop of titles each spring and fall.

Visit us on the Web at
www.cidermillpress.com
or write to us at
12 Port Farm Road
Kennebunkport, Maine 04046